*Dear Parent:*
*Your child's love of reading*

Every child learns to read in a different way [and at his or her own] speed. Some go back and forth between rea[ding levels and read] favourite books again and again. Others read through each level in order. You can help your young reader improve and become more confident by encouraging his or her own interests and abilities. From books your child reads with you to the first books he or she reads alone, there are I Can Read Books for every stage of reading:

**SHARED READING**
Basic language, word repetition, and whimsical illustrations, ideal for sharing with your emergent reader

**BEGINNING READING**
Short sentences, familiar words, and simple concepts for children eager to read on their own

**READING WITH HELP**
Engaging stories, longer sentences, and language play for developing readers

**READING ALONE**
Complex plots, challenging vocabulary, and high-interest topics for the independent reader

**ADVANCED READING**
Short paragraphs, chapters, and exciting themes for the perfect bridge to chapter books

**I Can Read Books** have introduced children to the joy of reading since 1957. Featuring award-winning authors and illustrators and a fabulous cast of beloved characters, I Can Read Books set the standard for beginning readers.

A lifetime of discovery begins with the magical words **"I Can Read!"**

*Visit www.icanread.ca for information*
*on enriching your child's reading experience.*

I Can Read Book® is a trademark of HarperCollins Publishers

*The Masked Man*
Text copyright © 2019 by HarperCollins Publishers Ltd.
Illustrations © 2019 by Nick Craine.
All rights reserved. Published by Collins, an imprint of HarperCollins Publishers Ltd

This work is adapted from a story of the same title in *5-Minute Hockey Stories* by Meg Braithwaite, illustrations by Nick Craine.
No part of this book may be used or reproduced in any manner whatsoever without the prior written permission of the publisher, except in the case of brief quotations embodied in reviews.

HarperCollins books may be purchased for educational, business, or sales promotional use through our Special Markets Department.

HarperCollins Publishers Ltd
Bay Adelaide Centre, East Tower
22 Adelaide Street West, 41st Floor
Toronto, Ontario, Canada
M5H 4E3

*www.harpercollins.ca*

Library and Archives Canada Cataloguing in Publication information is available upon request.

www.icanread.ca

ISBN 978-1-4434-5729-3

WZL 1 2 3 4 5 6 7 8 9 10

# THE MASKED MAN

by Meg Braithwaite

Illustrations by Nick Craine

Collins

In 1959, hockey was a scary game.

NHL players didn't wear helmets.

And goalies didn't wear masks.

It was a scary time.

Players zoomed around the ice,
chasing the puck.
Goalies stood tall in net,
just waiting to block a shot.

Lots of players got hurt.

They had no protection

for their heads and faces.

Finally, one Montreal Canadien
decided he'd had enough.
Jacques Plante wanted a change.

Jacques had been a goalie for
about ten years.

He'd been hurt many times.

He'd broken a lot of bones.

Jacques wanted to find a way

to protect his face.

Goalies had tried masks before.

None of them had worked.

Then something lucky happened.
One day, an inventor saw Jacques
get hit in the head with a puck.
He offered to make Jacques a mask.

The mask looked a little spooky.

But Jacques loved it.

He started to wear the mask

at every practice.

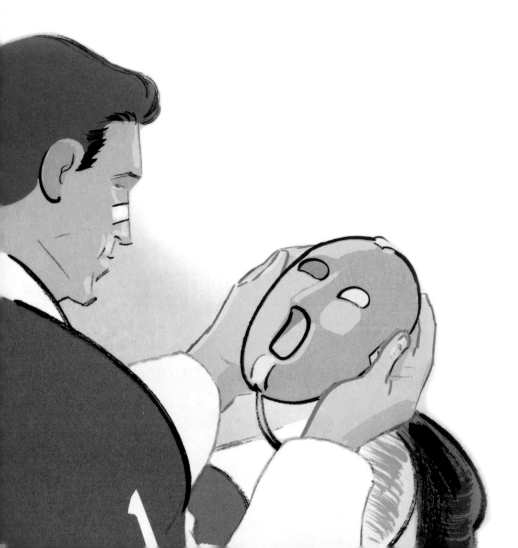

Jacques's coach did not
like the mask.

He thought goalies played better
when they were a little scared.

The coach told Jacques he couldn't wear his mask in real games. Jacques wasn't happy.

Then, during one game, a puck hit
Jacques right in the face.
It hit him really hard.

The puck cut Jacques's face and broke his nose.

Jacques skated off the ice.

He went to the locker room.

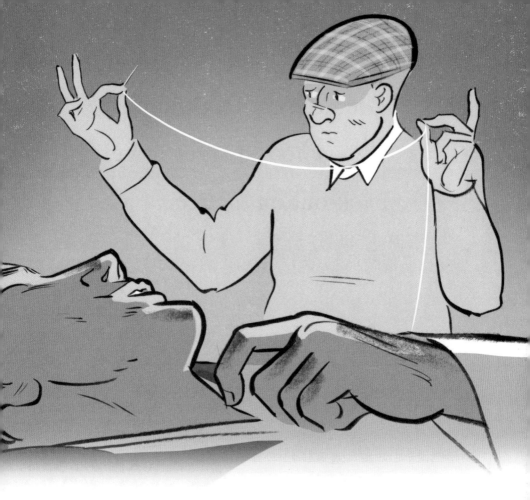

A doctor taped Jacques's nose and
sewed up his cut.
It took seven stitches.

Then the coach came in.
He wanted Jacques to get
back out on the ice.

The game needed to go on.

But Jacques said no.

"I won't play," Jacques said.

"Unless I can wear my mask."

The coach was very angry.

Outside the locker room,

the clock was ticking.

The players and fans were waiting

for the game to start again.

Finally, the coach made a decision.

"Okay," he said to Jacques.

"You can wear the mask this time."

Jacques skated back onto the ice.

He was wearing his mask.

Everyone was shocked.

They thought Jacques looked strange.

They thought he looked silly.

But then something great happened.

Jacques played so well that

the Canadiens won the game.

They won the next game too.

Jacques and the Canadiens

won eleven games in a row.

By then Jacques's cut had healed.

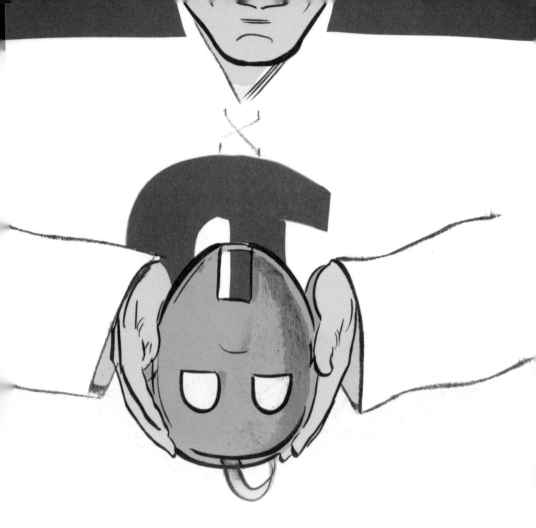

Lots of people were teasing him about wearing the mask.

Jacques didn't care.

He liked his mask.

But his coach still didn't like it.

So, in the next game,

Jacques played without his mask.

The Canadiens lost.

The coach wanted to win.

The team wanted to win.

The fans wanted to win!

So the coach let Jacques

wear the mask again.

It worked!

The Canadiens started to win again.

They even won the Stanley Cup.

Soon, other goalies
started wearing masks.

Today all players wear helmets.

All goalies wear masks.

And we have a goalie named

Jacques Plante to thank!